Facing Difficulties in Christian Family Life

by
Peter Kahn

All booklets are published thanks to the
generous support of the members of the
Catholic Truth Society

CATHOLIC TRUTH SOCIETY
PUBLISHERS TO THE HOLY SEE

Contents

Permissions: Love One Another! Magazine for permission to use the two testimonies in this booklet: "How to make him stop drinking", Love One Another! Magazine, No. 15/2010, and "A precious gift", Love One Another! Magazine, No. 6/2005. www.loamagazine.org.

All rights reserved. First published 2015 by The Incorporated Catholic Truth Society, 40-46 Harleyford Road London SE11 5AY Tel: 020 7640 0042 Fax: 020 7640 0046. © 2015 The Incorporated Catholic Truth Society.

ISBN 978 1 78469 030 4

Introduction

When Dante wanted to describe the lowest reaches of hell in his epic poem *Inferno*, he turned to sins of betrayal. For Dante there was no worse sin than to betray an intimate relation. The jovial friar Alberigo of Faenza had two of his kinsmen murdered during a banquet. It was said that the sign made by the friar to the assassins was "Bring on the fruit". Dante tells that for this act of betrayal the friar received payment, date for fig (that is, a more expensive fruit in place of the cheaper figs, or punishment harsher than the crime), in the ninth circle of hell. Branca d'Oria, meanwhile, killed his father-in-law while he was a guest in Branca's house. His fate, too, was to be encased in a frozen crust of despair. Amongst all the desperate souls present in hell, these souls were assigned to the very last station, encountered as Dante concluded his tour of that forlorn place.

There is no doubt that sins committed within the family are hard to bear. What is there to say when faced by domestic abuse and adultery, or even just quarrels and unruly children? It seems barely possible for brothers and sisters, husbands and wives, to live at peace with each other over any extended period of time. The idea that a family might be united can seem remote indeed, the vision of Psalm 132 (133) a mirage: "How good and how pleasant it is, brothers dwelling in unity!"

Then there are the difficulties we experience from the frailty of the human body, whether illness, miscarriage, old age, disability and many more kinds besides. And when someone dies, then death takes its toll on those left behind. Families are also economic units, and some of the keenest challenges we face in family life arise from unemployment, poverty or debt. Who would not feel crushed by an inability to provide for those who are nearest and dearest? All of this occurs in an existence that is shared with others. What, then, when others treat us or our family members unfairly?

Families generally try to keep such difficulties to themselves. One of the effects of this is that we can each think our own family is unique in its woes. But when you look at the statistics, you quickly realise that heart-rending circumstances are the norm. While rates and levels vary from one country or situation to the next, we see astonishingly high amounts of divorce, debt, illness, unemployment, abuse, discrimination, and so on. One study a few years ago found that couples argue an *average* of 312 times a year. Every family has its own share of troubles.

This booklet is not a self-help guide. The intention is not to offer solutions to these many problems that we experience in our families. As an author, I wouldn't want to suggest that this booklet is likely to provide a straightforward "happy ending" to your difficulties. It is not possible to wish away our difficulties. Rather, the booklet is intended as a *God-help* guide. Its immediate purpose is to draw attention to ways that God has helped other families in the past. Is it possible to experience difficult family circumstance in any other way than through a crust of despair? Can we live in ways that do not involve lapsing into bitterness? As the booklet unfolds, we will look at each of the main sets of difficulties that we identified above, and see grounds for hope.

On one memorable occasion, Pope Benedict visited the Shroud of Turin. The shroud is a length of linen cloth that many hold to be the garment in which Christ was buried in the tomb. The Pope said that the shroud is an image of Christ, one that reminds us that God's voice echoed in the realm of death on Holy Saturday. The Pope went on to say:

> The unimaginable occurred: namely, Love penetrated "hell". Even in the extreme darkness of the most absolute human loneliness we may hear a voice that calls us and find a hand that takes ours and leads us out. Human beings live because they are loved and can love; and if love even penetrated the realm of death, then life also even reached there. In the hour of supreme solitude we shall never be alone.[1]

Are these words a truth that each one of us can actually experience, or are they the pious musings of a remote religious figurehead? Is it true that Christ can be present to us in our despair and isolation, and that he can lead us out of it? In the Gospels, Christ often reaches out to families who are in need, rather than just to individuals. The stories in this booklet, at least, tell of how others today have seen Christ be present alongside them in their darkness.

Disunity in the family

Martha and Mary. They were responsible for what we can call the most famous family row of all time.[2] Martha was preoccupied with the serving, while Mary was busy - with sitting and listening to Jesus. Martha was not impressed with her sister's negligence, and she asked Jesus to intervene. Jesus, though, wasn't interested in addressing the disagreement in any direct fashion. Rather, he pointed out that an awareness of his presence in their home was more important than anything else.

Treasure in a field

Quarrels in the home are certainly a common difficulty in family life. Is there any way to avoid the anger, temper, malice, abusive language, dirty talk or lies that so often accompany them?[3] Well, St Paul has something of an answer in his famous fifth chapter of Ephesians. In relation to the morals of the home as a whole, St Paul says: "Give way to one another in obedience to Christ." (*Ep* 5:21) Rather than suggesting that a wife should just do what her husband tells her, St John Paul identified in this teaching of the apostle a call to a mutual subjection between husband and wife. If a husband and wife were to give way to each other out of reverence for Christ, then marriage would be easy. But is there in fact a harder teaching in the entire New Testament? A husband and wife will inevitably have different perspectives on what needs to happen, as was the case for Martha and Mary. If one party simply tries to impose his or her will on the other, as often occurs, then what you have is conflict. But what if the difference were an occasion to look for Christ in this situation together? The aim would then not be either to reach a compromise or to have one person triumph over the other, but rather to recognise Christ's presence.

One way in which the presence of Christ has traditionally been identified is when we act for the good of someone else, especially for their long-term benefit or destiny. I have one idea about my daughter's education, say, and my wife has another idea. Do we just slug it out, with the stronger party taking the victory, at least until the next skirmish? An open discussion about the situation might lead to a new perspective that neither of you had imagined before - one that could involve, for instance, a commitment to doing more than essentially handing over your child's education to someone else. When you experience the wonder of an initial disagreement turning into a deep source of union, then you also long for this to recur. Even this longing is something precious in itself. We are united to each other in the depths of our desire more than anywhere else, and God certainly has a clear place in making this happen.

The challenge is to see what is good for another person. You can only ever really see this if you are willing to put your own interests in second place. It is a cause for wonder when you see a married couple living together in a way that is unified under Christ; just as it is a cause for sorrow when you see a couple who cannot give up their own wills for each other. It is hard to imagine that a quarrel-free marriage could be anything other than a work of God! "Faith" is the word that we use to describe our capacity to see God at work. A disagreement between a husband and wife is a field within which to search for buried treasure. I don't have a recipe to tell you how to hold different perspectives in tension while you look for Christ, but *if* a couple long for Christ to manifest himself in the situation, then Christ never disappoints.

The obvious retort to this perhaps pious-sounding lecture is that it is often the case that only one party is ever willing to give way, and what happens then? This is an absolutely central question for many difficulties in marriage, although it remains the case that a husband and wife can both hold this view at the same time. It is, of course, possible that God never did join the couple together, and that the marriage was null and void from the very beginning. The Church does indeed reserve the right to declare that a marriage never actually existed, as when the consent of the couple was marred by coercion or a grave external fear. You would not then necessarily expect to see such a depth of unity actually present within the relationship. I want to respond to this challenge of one party's intransigence more fully, though, by letting Teresa tell her story, an archetypal story. I make no apology for the fact that it follows a classic line. It demonstrates that human frailty complicates matters, and that others don't necessarily change easily.

How to make him stop drinking[4]

I have been married to an alcoholic for over thirty years. My husband's addiction developed over the course of many years, but somehow I did not notice it until it was too late. I lived with him, raised three children, and all this time, my number one enemy - alcohol - was never far away. Matters went from bad to worse. My husband left one job, and then another. Finally, after taking early retirement, he resigned from his family responsibilities altogether.

I wanted very much to help him. I know now that all my efforts were in vain: berating him when he came home late and drunk, going through his pockets, searching the cupboards and garage and destroying his stashes of alcohol, hiding the results of his drinking from the world, having the car repaired from damage incurred by his driving when drunk, etc., etc. All this only made matters worse. All I was doing was shielding him from the consequences of his disease. Not having to take responsibility for his condition, he had no reason to seek help for it. Twice he entered a secure ward for treatment, but he left after two or three months without benefitting from the help offered there. He took no constructive steps, such as contacting an AA group.

I eventually joined Al-Anon with but one aim in mind: to help him. I wanted to find the solution to his problem, to discover what I had to do to make him stop drinking. For three years I went as far as the doors of the local Al-Anon centre. I would study the meeting times and then walk away, only to return and hover at the doors again. Something drew me there - no doubt a sense of my own helplessness and impotence.

Finally, just over two years ago, I entered those "terrible doors" with a sense of overwhelming loss, helplessness, and shame. "What?" - I said to myself, "What, me, a woman with a university degree, working at a responsible job, having to admit that I am unable to cope with life, that my husband is an alcoholic, and that I am powerless to help him?" And then the uncertainty: "Who will I meet there? Wives of alcoholics? Will we have a language in common? How can they possibly help me?"

And yet what I found in that group, and what that group gave me, was a true miracle. What I found were women who had been wounded emotionally - sometimes physically - by alcoholics. I found friends, who on hearing my first word and seeing my first tear, supported me and showed me how to grow in my situation. I learned that alcoholism was an incurable and mortal disease; that there was no prescription to changing my husband; that I could change - and had to change - only myself; and that by changing myself, I could exert influence on those around me, including my alcoholic husband and wounded children.

Thanks to our weekly meetings, I am still learning things. No one tells me what I have to do. Each of us talks only about her own life and experiences. That is what I do - sometimes with a smile, sometimes with a suppressed sob in my throat. Every time, we pray anew the serenity prayer: "God grant me the serenity to accept the things I cannot change, courage to change the things I can, and wisdom to know the difference." Sometimes I say the same thing in my own words: "Lord, save me from meddling in things over which I have no control. Keep me at a safe distance from them, so that I may not be wounded again. Lord, help me not to overlook the things that depend on me and require my active attention. Help me not to leave unassisted anyone I have the power to help. Lord, grant me your wisdom, that I may distinguish between those things that require my action and those over which I have no control."

Apart from attending regular Al-Anon meetings, I have also gone on pilgrimages and attended spiritual retreats at my parish and elsewhere. In addition, I have undergone co-dependency therapy. All this is thanks to my Al-Anon friends who have become my second family. Nowhere else could I find the kind of support that they are able to give me. I know that if in the middle of the night I were to find myself at the door of any one of them, I would have only to knock and the door would be opened. And there I would find help, understanding, and a receptive heart.

As for my domestic situation, I am trying to isolate myself from the disease, even though I continue to live under the same roof with the man whom I love as my husband. My own suffering has also brought me closer to God. What would my faith be like, if I were not always praying for the healing of my husband in body and soul? I pray for his conversion. Although he was raised in a Catholic family, he continues to wage his private war with God. I persevere, knowing that not my will, but God's, will decide our future.

Seeing the families of sober alcoholics is a source of great hope for me. Loving marriages do survive the nightmare of alcoholism without falling apart. You can hear these couples give witness talks at meetings, retreats, and pilgrimages. They are living proof that it is possible. God's grace is great and his paths unknown. "Lord, grant me the serenity…"

Two poles of life

We cannot always understand why God allows certain things to happen, but, whatever the situation, Christ is there with you if you have the eyes to see him. For Teresa, Christ's presence manifested itself in a call to prayer and in union with others. But even if a separation from your spouse seems the only realistic course of action, Christ asks us to sacrifice our own interests for the other. The Church does indeed teach that someone has a straightforward right to separate from his or her spouse if a grave danger exists to one's body or soul, or to the children, or if the spouse makes their life in common unduly difficult.[5] It is helpful here to remember Pope Francis's advice: "Children and the elderly are the two poles of life and the most vulnerable as well, often the most forgotten."[6] But it is true also that if the reason for the separation no longer pertains, then the couple should come back together again.

This latter course of action - to come back together after the immediate reason for a separation has perhaps faded away over time - might seem difficult in itself. Christ did not become man to live from an autonomous will, to get what he wanted in life. He came down to earth to live from the will of his Father. If we simply expect our husband and wife to completely fulfil us in a marriage, then we are bound to be disappointed. Pope Benedict, in turn, has sound advice for us:

> Not even the beloved is capable of satisfying the desire that dwells in the human heart…every good experienced by man projects him toward the mystery that surrounds

the human being; every desire that springs up in the human heart echoes a fundamental desire that is never fully satisfied…[7]

God is in charge

Similar perspectives apply to how parents relate to their children. The context of the fifth chapter of Ephesians is clear that the sentence "Give way to one another in obedience to Christ" applies to parents and children, as much as it does to husbands and wives. Now that is something to think about! We are used to the idea that children should obey their parents. Parents, though, aren't just supposed to force their own will on their children. Parents generally have preferences as to how their son or daughter should behave, but St Paul effectively says that there may be times when a parent will recognise the presence of Christ, and give way to their son or daughter as a result! There is hope for family life if, by our own example, we can teach our children to give way in obedience to Christ.

A story reminds us that we can only expect to have this happen if we begin to learn from the inside that giving way in obedience to Christ leads to a deep source of satisfaction.

We had adopted a young girl, who had been affected by her mother's drug-taking during pregnancy. The adoption proved difficult for our eleven-year old lad, Michael. Mealtimes shifted from a quiet (if somewhat grunted) discussion into a wave of demands, noise, mess, impatience and tantrums. At first Michael got drawn into a niggled reaction to the focus on her needs. He then started to miss out on more and more meals. "Patience" was all we could say to him. "Watch her grow". "Just imagine what it will be like in a year's time when there is this bond between you, and she has seen you bear with her day after day. Nothing else in life will beat that!" "What is it like even now, when she is in a good mood?"

Another couple tell their story:

Our daughter Mariana had become pregnant as an unmarried teenager. We thought that we had had our fill looking after young children, but no, someone else had other plans in mind for at least some of our later years. Life was supposed to be different, with freedom to go out when we pleased and to travel to places we had not visited before, rather than to order our lives any longer around someone else's needs. Of course, Mariana and her little boy stay over frequently with us now, especially when a babysitting service is needed. And money is in short supply in that household. At times we have wondered about how much we should say, "This is your problem, get on with it." But there is no argument when the little lad is actually in our company. What more could we want more deeply in life than for him to grow up well?

Is there anything that fulfils a couple more deeply than acting for the good of their child, or in this case their grandchild? All of this is a gift from God. He is the one who ultimately disposes in these matters. But we can see why infertility is such a cross for a couple to bear. A married couple in this situation might do well to consider NaPro Technology as a way forward. This approach is based on understanding the individual woman's natural fertility cycle. If one takes into account the full range of patient diagnoses pertaining to infertility, across all relevant ages, then the overall chance of a having a child is around 50%. And there is even a reasonable chance that a couple who have previously failed with In Vitro Fertilisation will have a successful pregnancy with NaPro Technology.

Who is looking after the Ark?

Reverence for Christ with one's sons and daughters, though, has its own demands; and this is one reason why no one can claim a right to have a child. There is a story in the First Book of Samuel that tells of how one father heard God speak to him through prophets in relation to how he was bringing up his sons:

> Now the sons of Eli were scoundrels; they cared nothing for the Lord nor for the rights of the priests as regards the people. Whenever a man offered a sacrifice, the priest's servant would come with a three-pronged fork in his hand while the meat was being cooked; he would thrust

this into cauldron or pan, or dish or pot, and the priest claimed for his own whatever the fork brought up. That was how they behaved with all the Israelites who came there to Shiloh. The priest's servant would even come up before the fat had been burnt and say to the man who was making the sacrifice, "Give the priest meat for him to roast. He will not take boiled meat from you, but raw." Then if the man replied, "Let them first burn the fat and then take for yourself whatever you wish", he would retort, "No! You must give it to me now or I will take it by force". This sin of the young men was very great in the sight of the Lord, because they treated the offering made to the Lord with contempt. (*1 S* 2:12-17)

The account goes on to say that a prophet was sent by God to ask Eli to correct his sons. Samuel too, even though he was a young boy, was given a word from God to warn Eli of what would happen to his family. Eli's sons had decided to chart their own way in life. It seems that Eli would have preferred them to act differently, but he failed to correct them. He remained passive. Once their sinful habits had become fully established, Eli was not able to find the means to draw them back to the Lord. And, certainly, once a young person becomes set in their ways it can seem impossible to shift them. The things that our children long for above all else, whether the satisfactions of the appetite in the case of Eli's sons, or a disregard for anything but the stimulation of gaming or socialising online, can set as quickly and firmly as concrete. The day came when Eli heard the news that the Ark of the Covenant, which he had left in the care of his sons, had been captured by the Philistines. His sons had been killed as well. The scriptures then tell us, "Eli fell backward off his seat by the gate; his neck was broken and he died, for he was old and heavy." (*1 S* 4:18)

There is a fascinating sequel to Eli's story. There came a day when Samuel's own sons began to take bribes after starting to act as judges in Israel. The Biblical account clearly implies that once this became apparent they were removed from their role as judges. Samuel appointed a king instead, Saul, to rule over the people of Israel in preference to corrupt judges. Unlike Eli, Samuel remained in God's favour even though his sons also rebelled against God. The difference was that he acted, while Eli did not lift a finger. God doesn't expect us to force our children to live in a righteous manner, but he does expect us to act for their good. (Similarly, God doesn't necessarily expect us to convert our spouse if they have become intransigent, but he does still ask us to act for their good.)

There are few things harder for a mother or father, or indeed for other family members, when a young person begins to abandon their faith. This story is played out in many, many homes. God expects us to respond to such a situation with hope, rather than to lapse into passivity in the face of the inevitable. What hope is there, you might ask? Hope manifests itself in prayer, indeed, but also in pondering what might realistically help a son or daughter to see what actually brings deep satisfaction. A tenderness for our offspring is essential, even a tender welcome for a prodigal son or daughter after many years of waiting and longing. Hope holds out for an intervention from God. Perhaps your children will be eternally grateful to you if the practice of the Sacrament of Confession is established early in your family life. God takes the initiative at certain points in time, and this sacrament is one of those places where it is guaranteed to happen.

There is no magic pill here to make a child obedient or to make a spouse see reason, even in cases where they are manifestly choosing something that harms the rest of the family. For many people this constitutes a reason to doubt the existence of God. One of the great blessings of Pope Benedict's ministry was the scale of his wisdom. I make no apology for mining the inheritance he has left us:

> However, let us ask ourselves: how is it possible to think of an omnipotent God while looking at the Cross of Christ? At this power of evil which went so far as to kill the Son of God? Naturally, what we would like would be a divine mightiness that fitted our own mindset and wishes: an "omnipotent" God who solves problems, who intervenes to prevent us from encountering difficulties, who overcomes adverse powers, changes the course of events and eliminates suffering. Thus today various

theologians say that God cannot be omnipotent, for otherwise there would not be so much suffering, so much evil in the world. In fact, in the face of evil and suffering, for many, for us, it becomes problematic, difficult, to believe in a God who is Father and to believe that he is omnipotent; some seek refuge in idols, succumbing to the temptation to seek an answer in a presumed "magic" omnipotence and its illusory promises. Nevertheless faith in almighty God impels us to have a very different approach: to learn to know that God's thought is different from our own, that God's ways are different from ours (cf. *Is* 55:8) and that his omnipotence is also different."[8]

How does God speak to us?

We can't expect a prophet to roll up at our door and give us a word from God. The Letter to the Hebrews tells us that in the past God spoke to our forefathers through the prophets, but that in these last days he has spoken to us through his Son. What we can expect is for deep desires for the good of our son or daughter to well up within the depths of our hearts. The game-changer with the coming of Christ is that we have received the gift of the Holy Spirit through the Church.

The Church is sometimes seen as *the* source of difficulties themselves in family life: "Do this"; "You can't do that." But actions we might want to undertake in opposition to the teaching of the Church will not in themselves heal our brokenness. A new marriage may provide many things, but why should it teach you how to give up your own will? St Augustine said that the entire history of the world boils down to a struggle between two kinds of love: self-love to the point of hatred for God, and love of God to the point of self-renunciation. He said that it is the second form of love that saves both the world and the self. St Paul similarly gives just two options: either we look to our own selfish interests, or we look to the interests of others (see *Ph* 2:3-4). It is true that our own interests will not always be selfish ones, but if a focus on our own interests dominates, then selfishness usually follows closely behind. If you downplay the interests of your children and your spouse, why should this lead to self-forgetfulness?

The frailties of the human body

Paul was working on a job in his house, one that his wife had been asking him to do for a while. He had been rushing things in order to get it out of the way. Somehow he managed to fall over and break his leg. The nurse who took off his cast at the hospital was intrigued why as a builder he hadn't been devastated by the injury. After all, the broken leg had meant no work for a couple of months, and no income. "Why are you like this?" she asked. Paul had just talked about the people he had met at the food bank. For some reason they had started going out for a drink together. He'd never had time to make local friends before, so this was something of a novelty. The enjoyment seemed to over-ride the misery of the broken leg.

This is the first of a set of stories in this section. What we will see in each of these stories is that both wretchedness and consolation can occur together. An occasion of desolation can become the means for solace, even if the source of that desolation remains. For Paul in the above story, it wasn't as if a new source of income suddenly materialised, but nonetheless his experience was different. In each of the stories that follow it is clear that the frailty of the human body means that an individual cannot control even just his or her own life in its entirety. Perhaps this should not come as such a surprise, since we did not give ourselves an existence in the first place! What we can do, though, is be present in the circumstances that we encounter with an eye that is open to the eternal good of others, or with a firm desire for an encounter with Christ. We cannot control what happens to us, even in those things that seem to matter more than anything else, but we can recognise the Mystery at work. If we hold our desire for Christ open - looking for something new, for an opportunity to encounter someone else - then the Mystery can reach out to us.

Amanda tells her story:

We had longed for this baby, but everything seemed to fall apart after the child arrived in my womb. Morning sickness seemed so ineptly named; it was twenty-four hours a day. How would I survive with a husband at work and the other children still so demanding? But, perversely, the sickness itself turned out to be a source of vast comfort. It prevented me from forgetting that I was pregnant and that there was a child present within me. I had spent my first pregnancy complaining, even though little had gone wrong. The awareness became almost continual. What would he or she be like? Just imagine, another little body nestling next to me in bed, growing up into so many interests. What an incredible gift! My husband and I certainly couldn't create such a life on our own.

One couple found that a miscarriage could be an occasion for both searing pain and profound consolation, side by side. Cristina began to undergo a miscarriage while her husband Sergio was away. The husband of a friend to whom she turned offered to undertake a four-hour drive to collect him if this would help. In the event the offer was not needed, but the gesture itself demonstrated how much her friend realised the pain she was experiencing, and this in itself offered some consolation. The miscarriage itself did occur shortly afterwards, with Cristina's own life in danger at one point. The couple had experienced two previous miscarriages before, and each time they had primarily experienced simply a dulling of pain and loss over time. But this time the experience was different. Rather than remain passive in the face of this pain, they were reminded by an exchange of emails with another friend that one can hope for the eternal salvation of a child who has died in the womb. The Church teaches that we cannot be certain of such a person's salvation, but that a hope remains to us. Fortunately, you can give expression to a hope. The couple found a deep consolation in naming their child during a Rite of Committal from the Church's *Order of Christian Funerals*, and in praying for the eternal salvation of all their miscarried children and offering the sacrifice of the Mass for their good. You might think that such religious devotion would provide merely a thin consolation in the face of such a loss, but this was not their experience.

And then John's story:

My wife had died, and I was left with our young daughter. Others around us have been deeply moved, to spend time with us. We have even been accompanied by others on visits to her grave. I cannot understand why it happened this way. People spent time with us - it was as if Christ himself had come to spend time with me and my daughter. The other side of the bed next to me remained empty, and the tears still continued to flow. But I had never realised before that such a depth of bond could exist outside of my immediate family. I had never imagined that my relations with others beyond the family could be based on anything more than largely functional interactions. Each day begins for me with a sense of wonder - who will it be who reaches out to me today, or who can I reach out to in my own turn now that I have warmed to others? Each day has become a gift.

Naomi's daughter had been born with Down's Syndrome. There were so many appointments, tests and treatments to go through, whether it was the physiotherapist or the paediatrician, the cardiologist or the Health Visitor. She became aware that anxiety and worry were beginning to become a dominant note in her life. What would happen if this situation was to arise, or that eventuality was to occur? One day she realised that she found a measure of peace in her situation when she stopped just mulling over the condition itself, and began to think of ways to express her love through concrete acts of generosity for her child. What would be of help, and how could she provide it? Rather than remain somewhat passive while she allowed professionals to offer their care, excellent as it was, she realised that she had scope for a much more active part of her own. Each circumstance offered different possibilities for her daughter, for acts of love. Quite naturally she found that they spent more time simply enjoying each other's company, whether it was noticing the birdsong or driving together to an appointment.

Alan's wife, Siobhan, had a job that took her away from home at times, and away from their three young children. The hardest point in the day for Alan was always at bedtime, when everyone's tiredness levels were sky-high. He had to deal with the endless procrastinations, the crying, and the unwillingness to respond to simple commands. Everything was much calmer when Siobhan was there for the usual routine. None of them, certainly, looked forward to the times when she was away, even though they had relatively little control over the frequency or timing of her absences. One day, though, Alan realised that his wife took much more time with the children at bedtime. She rarely rushed them, but evidently seemed just to enjoy the little tasks and stories. It occurred to him that a child is not a machine that you can just turn off at the end of day, for it to recharge overnight. When Siobhan was away particularly, he realised that his own tasks and preoccupations would need to wait, so he could give his children more attention. Telling bedtime stories to his children was undoubtedly more enchanting than shouting at them. In time a greater tenderness for his children began to emerge, even alongside the tiredness and the whines.

Christ reaching out to families

We see similar perspectives in the Scriptures. There is the story of Hannah earlier in the Book of Samuel. A man called Elkanah son of Jeroham had two wives, Hannah and Peninnah. We are told that Peninnah had plenty of children, but that Hannah was barren. Hannah had to face one difficulty that Christians today, at least, won't encounter. Her husband's other wife used to taunt and provoke her because she had no children. One year we find that it all became too much for Hannah. On the annual visit to the temple of the Lord at Shiloh, she refused to eat from the meal that they took after the sacrifice. She then went into the Temple to pour out her heart to God: "In the bitterness of her soul she prayed to the Lord with many tears." (*1 S* 1:10) The priest Eli at first thought she was drunk, but she told him that she had been pouring out her soul to God. She had been praying for a son, promising to give him over to God for his entire life. Eli, as a priest, stood in the place of Christ as he interceded with God for her request. Even before she bore her son she was dejected no longer by her circumstances.

When we turn to the Gospels we see that Christ does not simply intercede for us in our difficulties with his Father, but that he himself is deeply moved by our plight. What is more, Christ particularly reaches out to those who are most deeply moved for the sake of their children. Christ was compassionate to the tears of the widow of Nain, whose only son had died. Her tears provoked a response in Christ's own heart, as he felt sorry for her. "Don't cry," he said, before going on to raise her son from the dead. In doing so, he repeated the action of the prophet Elijah, who had also raised to life the only son of a widow. When a child is an only son or daughter, then the desire of the father or mother is even keener. We see in Luke chapter nine that a man with a son who was suffering from epilepsy "implored" Jesus to cure his son. In John chapter four, there was a royal official whose son was ill. He travelled a long way to seek out Jesus, asking him to come and cure his son. Jesus tested his resolve and his faith, by pointing out that signs and portents were an insufficient basis for faith, but the man did not give up on his plea. Salvation came to the royal official's entire family as a result of his faith.

Luke tells the story of Jairus,[9] who was the president of a synagogue. We see the depth of his desire as he pleads with Jesus to come to his house in order to heal his only daughter who was dying. Even as Jesus began to make his way to the young girl, a message came that she had died. By all normal standards, there would be nothing more that

Jesus could now do for her. But Jesus continued into the house along with his three intimate disciples. He threw out those were crying and mourning, even as they ridiculed him for suggesting that the girl was not dead but asleep. We hear that Jesus then took the little girl by the hand and said to her, "Child, get up." Her spirit returned and she got up. The astonishment of her parents must have been great indeed.

Each of these occasions of difficulty was for the parents an occasion to be moved very deeply, and to encounter Christ. Christ did not enter the house of every young child who had just died in Israel. We need to give expression to the desires that lie within our hearts, and to become protagonists as we reach out to Christ. In the sufferings that we each experience, we see our inability to provide what is most truly needed for our children. It is here that we can encounter Christ. He only entered Jairus's house after an urgent request. It is in the depth of our desire for our families that we find Christ. We see this in the story that now follows from Denise. How do you cope in life, and to whom do you turn, when two of your three children are diagnosed with a life-threatening illness?

A Precious Gift[10]

Our eldest son Ian was born healthy. When David was born thirteen months later with multiple problems, including a cleft lip, paralysis affecting his right side, and, more seriously, severe aplastic anemia, life took a more difficult turn. Hannah was born five years later. She was also diagnosed with severe aplastic anemia. The prognosis for both of them was devastating. Without the gift of a bone-marrow transplant, children with severe aplastic anemia rarely live beyond their teenage years.

Both children were now fighting for their lives, alternating between being tied to endless blood transfusions (to stabilise their condition and keep them alive in the short term) and going into brief periods of remission. David was the first to go into remission, which was just as well, as I had my hands full with baby Hannah; she required six blood transfusions a week.

I struggled on a day-to-day basis just to keep going. Some mornings I could scarcely face the day. Everything was sheer effort. Seeing my inner turmoil, my doctor offered me medication to help pull me through; but, whether I was just stubborn or unable to evaluate the state of my emotional and mental health, I refused the medication. There had to be another answer somewhere.

One morning I walked the boys to school. I was feeling particularly low and avoided eye contact with the other mothers in the playground. I was tired of having to answer the same questions about Hannah's health. On my way home, I passed by the gates of our parish church. I suddenly felt irresistibly drawn into the church. I just wanted to sit there in the silence, and pray. Reversing the pram, I wheeled it inside the gates, and carried Hannah into the porch. Holy Mass was almost over. I crept inside and sat down at the back of the church. Hannah gurgled happily over my shoulder.

At first I panicked, thinking that the elderly ladies would rush over after Mass and inquire about Hannah. I was in no mood for talk, so I lowered my head as they left. I closed my eyes, and from deep within I felt this overwhelming cry to God. My soul seemed to soar to God. "Please, please, help me. I can't manage this on my own," I screamed interiorly to my heavenly Father. And, in this one moment, I surrendered totally to God. I recognised my utter dependency on him. Wholly absorbed, I did not notice that our parish priest had sat down beside me on the bench. I tried to ignore him, hoping he would take the hint and leave. I resented the intrusion. Finally, I looked up into his face. "Denise, I have been sitting here waiting. What's wrong?" he asked.

What's wrong!" I thought. I felt like screaming and pounding my fists against his chest. Instead I took a deep breath. Then I began to think that maybe God had placed him there for a reason. And I opened my heart to him. Everything poured out. On walking out of the church, I felt suddenly energised. Real joy and hope had entered my heart. Later I came to understand that this was my conversion experience.

I walked a "journey" with David, holding his little hand tightly. During that "journey," I began, in the deepest core of my being, to search out the very meaning of life. Strange as it may sound, suffering became the tool by which God drew me to himself. Suffering is not an idea that is in vogue. But slowly, very slowly, it became my teacher as it began to open up my spirit to surrender and reach out to God for his help when my own resources were completely exhausted. He responded to my need.

David had a special spirit that was coloured by a rainbow of experiences. Many of these life experiences had painful "dark" hues, but he used them to deepen in maturity, love and generosity. He lived an ordinary life, filled at times with pain and frustration, but also with moments of ecstatic joy and sheer exuberance over a life fully lived. Joy is to be found even at the darkest of times.

In the final weeks of David's short life, I began to notice subtle changes in his personality. Physically, he was fading away before our very eyes. Lacking the vitality to tear around with his brother and sister, he grew resigned to this quieter period of his life. He accepted the limitations that his illness now placed on him. His serenity was matched by a growing spiritual maturity. It was almost as if he were "transfigured" before my eyes as he allowed God to fill him with his life and love. I felt in awe of the radiant grace transforming him. Truly he was holy ground. "Mum, I don't want to be attached to this drip on my tenth birthday," he blurted out one evening while undergoing a transfusion.

The Lord must have heard his plea. He was in heaven for his tenth birthday. At his packed Requiem Mass our parish priest told the congregation: "God permitted him to live a relatively short time, but it seemed that in that time he had done a lifetime's work. Despite his limp and his impish grin, David always seemed to be in a hurry. He was always on the run. He would never walk if he could possibly run. He has now run into the arms of Christ. It is not too often that little Davids pass through our world, but when they do, we ought to take time to appreciate them. They teach us about how life really is. They are the special loved ones of God."

When Hannah approached her tenth birthday she too began to fade. She was following the same path as David. An initial search on bone-marrow registers proved fruitless. However, a year later a donor did appear. Hannah received the "gift" of life thanks to a bone-marrow transplant from an unrelated donor.

The Lord has indeed pulled me from the dark pit into the light of his loving presence. More powerfully than I could have imagined, he continues to fill me with his peace and strength, and I thank him for this, day in and day out.

Jesus wept

As parents, the difficulties that our children experience touch us like nothing else. Many of the stories in this booklet relate to the challenges of bringing children into the world, and of living together with them. Stories on this theme crop up surprisingly frequently, more so it seems than stories on relationship difficulties between husbands and wives, say. Perhaps it is not a surprise that people are more willing to share stories of comfort in heartbreak than stories that pertain to their own sin or to the sin of another.

In these stories we learn what it means to cry out to God for our children. The frailness of our own bodies, and the bodies of our children, teaches us that we are designed to rely on God. The stories that we have included speak of the ways in which God acts, and how the difficulties we experience provide an occasion for us to recognise that we are not self-sufficient, and to cry out to God from the very depths of our being. It is only when we are moved in this way that we can truly expect God to hear our prayers. But we can become weary or cynical when we find our prayers do not seem to get answered. The *Catechism of the Catholic Church* quotes from the writings of St John Damascene to tell us that prayer is the raising of one's mind and heart to God or the requesting of good things from God. These two dimensions of prayer are closely entwined with each other.

After speaking of the nature of prayer, St John Damascene goes on in his own writing to remind us of the way that Our Lord prayed for Lazarus before the passion. Jesus makes a straightforward request for something good from his Father, namely that Lazarus will come out of the tomb. But Jesus's prayer is preceded by deep distress, profound sighing and weeping. We receive a clear sense in the Gospels that Martha, Mary and Lazarus were amongst Jesus's closest friends. In responding to their need, Jesus did not simply make a factual application, and leave everything else to his Father. Nor was he just working up an intense feeling that his prayer would be answered. Instead, the Holy Spirit moved the very depths of Jesus's being. The *Catechism* suggests that we know from part of his prayer for Lazarus ("I know that you always hear me") that Jesus "constantly made such petitions."[11] Jesus knew that as the Spirit moved his heart, so the Father would hear his prayer. The heart has a privileged place in the kingdom of heaven. If we each pray for those we encounter in life from our innermost being, then there is truly hope for our families.

In some ways there seems more hope for answered prayer where human frailty is concerned rather than human sin. After all, St Peter quite clearly suggests that if a husband and wife treat each other with consideration in their life together, then nothing will come in the way of their prayers. But if a couple shows each other disdain in their life together, then there will be many barriers to answered prayer.

The conversion of a hard heart requires a miracle indeed if it is to occur. Just imagine, Jeremiah had spent a lifetime prophesying to the people of Israel. Everything that he had said would happen, had happened. Not one of his words had fallen to the ground. And yet even after the fall of Jerusalem to King Nebuchadnezzar, those who were left behind refused to accept the words that he had for them. We are told that all the military leaders, and all of the people from the greatest to the least, approached Jeremiah and asked him to intercede with God so that they would know what to do. They asked Jeremiah *Ora pro nobis ad Dominum Deum nostrum* - "Pray for us to the Lord our God" (*Jr* 42:20). However, when Jeremiah then told them that the Lord wanted them to stay in the land of Israel, the people would have none of it. They wished to go to the "safety" of Egypt, away from the fate of their many relatives who had already suffered death and exile at the hands of the Chaldeans. The remaining body of people fled to Egypt, forcibly taking Jeremiah with them. We share the same human nature as these Israelites, and we too can ignore again and again the words that God sends to us.

And yet there is still hope for the conversion of wayward hearts within our families. Hope is certainly at its greatest when the one offering up endless prayers is a saint. There is the well-known story of St Augustine, with his mother Monica praying earnestly for his conversion for year after year, with many tears. She was married early in life to Patricius, who may have lived a dissolute and unfaithful life. Their son, Augustine, soon took after his father rather than his mother. It was only when Augustine was thirty-three years old that his heart changed. The circumstances that Monica encountered, indeed, became part of the means by which she was able to live such a generous life.

Providing for your family

Nikola was working part-time in a supermarket, and her hours were cut down. The family finances were already tight. What was she to do? At first she simply became angry, but after talking to a friend, she agreed that there was another option. The friend never simply nodded in agreement with her complaints. Nikola asked her "Why not?" "Those additional hours could still be a gift for you to spend time with your children." Even though she couldn't get her boss to increase her hours, she could take a longer-term view of the situation and work as well as she could. Who knows, her situation might change. Even though the family had to make do with a smaller income, she now remembers the difficulty as the time she first learnt to enjoy chatting with the customers while still clearing her queue at the checkout. Prior to that, her job had simply been a way of earning a wage. She now realises that God had given her something much more than just money in her pocket. Her difficulty became an occasion to encounter others.

We are in danger of creating a society in which no one relates to each other any longer. You receive services from others, but real human contact rarely forms part of the transaction. The widespread breakdown that we see in family relationships is part of our human condition at large. It is worth calling to mind what happened at the beginning of the world. Adam was informed by God as to the consequences of his sin as follows:

> Accursed be the soil because of you. With suffering shall you get your food from it every day of your life. It shall yield you brambles and thistles, and you shall eat wild plants. With sweat on your brow shall you eat your bread, until you return to the soil, as you were taken from it. For dust you are and to dust you shall return. (*Gn 3*:17-19)

This text does not imply that before the Fall the man would have worked with a dry brow under the heat of the sun. Indeed, St Thomas Aquinas is clear: "In paradise man would have been like an angel in his spirituality of mind, yet with an animal life in his body."[12] One can have the somewhat romantic notion that life before the Fall was one of ease and pleasure. But the *Catechism of the Catholic Church* speaks of Adam and Eve being created in a state of original holiness, rather than a state of perfection.[13] In light of these teachings, I would suggest that some form of hardship was originally intended for us by God, even if this was not to have been experienced as suffering. Many kinds of work have their own inherent challenges - these indeed make life interesting for us, whether it is the complexities of people's own aspirations and values, or the satisfaction in seeing a field of hard soil yielding to an inventive way of turning it over.

Jane was an Occupational Therapist. As each month went by there were fewer colleagues and more appointments. The pressure on the service seemed to be mounting endlessly. The stress began to affect her time at home with the family. She increasingly came home late, and struggled to rush the children off to school as early as possible each day. Clinics were more likely to over-run if she wasn't fully ready.

I became increasingly focused on handing out instructions for my clients to follow, rather than exploring at a little more depth what they were interested in taking on, or what might motivate them to adapt their lives. After all, it took less time to tell someone what they needed to do, even if I still followed normal practice in routinely writing down their own goals. It was one elderly lady who came back to me on a supposedly final appointment, candidly confiding to me that she wasn't really that interested in following my advice, who gave me pause for thought. It became clear that many of my patients needed time and attention to articulate or even become aware of their aspirations in life. The demands on the clinic never changed, but I began to rediscover my early enthusiasm for the work.

All of the circumstances that we experience remain in some clear way a gift to us from God, if we have the eyes to see this. One father sees this as follows:

Our teenage son Joe had been at a boarding school for a while now, but the funding arrangements had changed and he was now back at home. My wife and I had felt that we had failed as parents when we sent him off to this school that took young people on the autistic spectrum. We hadn't really been able to cope with the continual demands, especially when he took to banging doors at night. How would we cope now? We realised quite quickly that we would fail again if we simply tried to provide for his needs on our own. We had tried that route before and it had failed miserably. Who else there who might help? We had heard that there were new movements in the Church before this, but a friend in the parish happened to remark one day that she had never such attention to those with a disability as in this particular group. The thought came into my head, "Why hadn't I heard of this before?" But I realised that I had a choice, of responding in the present to the insight that had been offered to me or of wallowing in an age-long bitterness. I couldn't ever expect to be in control of the situation, so perhaps I could learn to be more receptive to the help that was out there.

There are factors that can make it nigh on impossible for us to provide for the needs of our families. Pope Francis, for instance, has spoken of the challenges faced by refugee and immigrant families, especially those who have been forced to migrate. On the Feast of the Holy Family, the Pope reminded us that the Gospel of the day presented the Holy Family to us as it sought refuge in Egypt: "Jesus wanted to belong to a family who experienced these hardships, so that no one would feel excluded from the loving closeness of God."[14] Even an experience of exploitation and exile can become an occasion to encounter Christ.

Fallout from society

It is not possible to control the actions of another or to force them to act in a certain way. Suffering is especially hard to bear when it is deliberately inflicted on us by others. After the Fall, God said to the woman that her husband would 'lord it' over her. The Hebrew word for this phrase "lord it", *mashal,* clearly includes the very real possibility that the husband will act as a tyrant. The word *mashal* in fact is frequently used in this sense in the Book of Isaiah. This is what life is like without God to intervene on our behalf, and this is often the reality of our lives. There are few things that are harder to bear than experiencing someone who has power over us using that power for our harm, or indeed for the harm of a family member. Perhaps that person is your own husband or wife, or your boss at work. It could be another child in the playground, a neighbour, or a teacher; as we see in this next story.

My daughter, Nidhi, had begun to have a hard time at school, as a teacher continually picked on her. The relentless antagonism expressed itself in the smallest of ways, but it never let up. We had thought of moving schools. Whatever she did there was a fault with it. It began to wear us down. The next time I had the opportunity to go to the school to meet my daughter's teachers I made a point of seeing this one teacher, as I surely couldn't just ignore the situation. Her face hardened a little as I sat down. I had an inspiration to ask her about her subject, "What interests you most of all in teaching this subject?" This wasn't the question that she was expecting! But then nor did she give an answer that we might have expected. We found at least some common ground, although we realised, too, that we came from different worlds. We spent the time just talking about the subject, rather than about my child's difficulties. I realised we couldn't force her to close down her antagonism, but we could try to make a connection with her, in a way that was independent from our daughter's difficulties. She would surely be a better teacher if she were more aware of her own enthusiasms for the subject. Something shifted in her after this meeting, even if there wasn't exactly a great deal of mutual sympathy.

The story of Jacob reminds us of the power that others can have over us. For twenty years, Jacob had lived away from his home in the Promised Land. During that time he had been able to do relatively little to avoid hardship at the hands of his uncle, Laban. Up to a point he had been able to act on his own behalf, by using some of his trickery. He had struck a deal with his uncle about which sheep he would own, and made sure that the strongest new sheep would all be his. But he had been unable to prevent endless sleepless nights, working in the devouring heat, or having to pay compensation when an animal was lost or mauled. The booklet entitled *Work and the Christian Family* (in this same series as this booklet) draws out the story further in relation to Jacob's work. He had slaved away for seven years to win the hand of his beloved, Rachel, but they had seemed to him like a few days because he loved her so much. However, much later on, Jacob decided to leave and return to his homeland. He fled, in fact, taking his family and his flocks with him. Laban was most put out, and decided to pursue him and seize what Jacob had taken. Laban caught up with Jacob, and clearly had the power to do him great harm. But on this occasion God intervened, appearing to Laban in a dream and telling him on no account to go against Jacob. And then shortly afterwards, we find Jacob had to meet his brother Esau, his enemy, who had with him four hundred armed men. Jacob felt very little control over the destiny of his family.

Why did God intervene in Jacob's life to save him? Why did he appear to Laban in a dream, and soften Esau's heart? Is there a hope here that God will also be able to intervene on our behalf as well? Despite his deceptions, Jacob had given his entire life over to God. This was evident when he married a girl from his mother's family rather than an idol-worshipping Canaanite woman, in how he worked so lovingly for the hand of Rachel in marriage, in the altars that he built whenever the Lord appeared to him; and in much more besides. We cannot save ourselves or our families. What we can do is maintain a deep relation with God, and respond to the initiative that he takes on our behalf. There is a fascinating German study which found, for the couples considered, that half of the couples who either married in a state institution or just cohabited broke up.[15] The figure was 33% for couples who had married in church, and 2% for couples who attended Mass each Sunday. However, for couples who prayed together every day and attended Mass each Sunday, the figure was 0.07%. A bond with Christ strengthens the bond between a husband and wife.

We see something similar to Jacob's situation with his son, Joseph. He was sold by his brothers into slavery in Egypt. Joseph accepted the injustices that came to him without becoming bitter. He respected God as the author of reality. And then when he had worked his way up as a slave in the household of Potiphar, he found Potiphar's wife in her turn looking to impose her will on him. He remained faithful to God in this temptation. His brothers might sell him into slavery, and Potiphar's wife have him thrown into prison, but in neither case did Joseph become bitter. God did not intervene straight away to free Joseph from the oppression of slavery and imprisonment. In this respect, God allowed events to take their course. Joseph certainly suffered a great deal. God intervened in his own good time, and in a way that brought salvation to Jacob's entire family. It was through Joseph's suffering that God formed a people who were to relate to each other, through seeking to be generous towards each other rather than dominating each other.

At the end of his life, Joseph was able to perceive that his own suffering had led to a great grace for his family, as he told his brothers: "Do not reproach yourselves for having sold me here, since God sent me before you to preserve your lives." (*Gn* 45:5) God has something more for Joseph than he could ever have imagined, something that he had to wait for in order to experience. When Joseph looked at his suffering he did not see the evil of his brothers, but the goodness of God. Sorrows that are borne with the Spirit of God, and with love, are no longer the burdens they might have been. God used Joseph's suffering to bring Jacob's entire family to Egypt, and to save them from death during a great famine. We cannot expect that God will wave our difficulties away, but if we have Jacob's trust in God, and Joseph's awareness of God's presence, then we will see the redemption of our families.

It might seem easier to accept our human frailties as opportunities to recognise God's gifts to us, at least in comparison to suffering that comes to us from the hands of others. But Joseph's story says that even this is possible, too. This is in indeed an instance of the cross. Christ himself came to his own people, to his family, and was rejected by the people of Israel. Can there be any more heartbreaking story in the whole of human history? There is no promise at all that our difficulties will, humanly speaking, be resolved. But if the gift of faith accompanies this suffering, then there is hope that others will come to life as a result.

Conclusion

It is intriguing that the effects of the Fall are partly overwritten in these stories of Jacob and Joseph. Their work was actually fruitful and fulfilling, even if it involved sleepless nights and slavery. When others tried to lord it over them, God intervened in his own good time. Death did not result in the way that you might have imagined it would. We will never be able to experience life quite as Adam and Eve knew it. Nonetheless, Pope Benedict is clear that we can still receive back something of what was once lost. In commenting on the parable of the prodigal son, he indicates:

> In the parable, the father orders the servants to bring quickly "the first robe". For the Fathers, this "first robe" is a reference to the lost robe of grace with which man had been originally clothed, but which he forfeited by sin. But now this "first robe" is given back to him - the robe of the son.[16]

In the Letter to the Colossians, St Paul compares the life of charity to a garment.[17] We cannot control the actions of others in any direct sense, whether the person concerned is a husband, wife, child, brother, sister or whoever. What each of us can do, though, is to receive this lost robe of grace. Jacob and Esau made different choices. We each have a choice to make in how we respond to the difficulties that we encounter in our lives.

It is intriguing that family relationships figure closely in Dante's account of the heights of heaven in his poem *Paradiso*, just before he experiences the beatific vision. Our Lady's mother, Anna, is seated next to St Peter. She gazes with a self-forgetful happiness at her daughter, not even moving her eyes. Dante also picks out the wives of the patriarchs for special attention: Rachel, Sarah and Rebecca. Rachel is seated next to the great heroine of the *Divine Comedy* as a whole, Beatrice, who leads Dante through the different spheres of heaven. It is truly a source of great wonder to see family members at one with each other. For Dante the experience then helps him gaze towards the radiance of the first Love.

A return to family relationships as God intended them in the beginning of time might seem a little far-fetched. All of the stories in this booklet either testify to experiences that others have had, or they have been inspired and crafted on the basis of such experiences. When human frailty and sin combine together, then the suffering is intense indeed. But if we make our own the mind of Christ, then unity with others is possible. At no point in the Gospels do we see Christ wrapped up in his own preoccupations. His eye gazes outwards, to his Father and to those around him. We cannot control our circumstances, but we can be patient as we long for Christ to reach out to us as we encounter difficulties.

Endnotes

[1] Pope Benedict XVI, Pastoral Visit to Turin, Veneration of the Holy Shroud: Meditation, 2nd May 2010.

[2] Lk 10:38-42.

[3] Col 3:8-9.

[4] "How to make him stop drinking", *Love One Another! Magazine*, No. 15/2010, www.loamagazine.org.

[5] *Code of Canon Law*, Book IV, Part I, Chapter 9, Article 2, Canons 1151-1155.

[6] Pope Francis, "Address to Participants in the Plenary Assembly of the Pontifical Council for the Family", 25th October 2013.

[7] Pope Benedict XVI, General Audience, 7th November 2012.

[8] Pope Benedict XVI, General Audience, 30th January 2013.

[9] Lk 8:40-56.

[10] "A precious gift", *Love One Another! Magazine*, No. 6/2005, www.loamagazine.org.

[11] *Catechism of the Catholic Church (CCC)* par. 2604.

[12] St Thomas Aquinas, *Summa Theologica*, 1, Q. 98, a. 2. 1., www.newadvent.org/summa/1098.htm.

[13] CCC par. 399.

[14] Pope Francis, Angelus, Feast of the Holy Family of Nazareth, 29th December 2013.

[15] *Das Gebet, Schlussel der Heiligkeit*, "Der Fels", No. 11/2002, p. 325.

[16] Pope Benedict XVI, *Jesus of Nazareth* (London, Bloomsbury, 2007), p. 206.

[17] Col 3:12-14.

Faith in the Family

Anne Burke-Gaffney & Fr Marcus Holden

Faith in the Family is a handbook for parents, helping them transmit key aspects of the faith to their children.

Divided into three themes: 'Creation and created', 'Knowing God' and 'Catholic life and times', questions and answers are expressed in language that can be easily communicated by parents to children and then translated into action and supported with prayers, activities and practical suggestions.

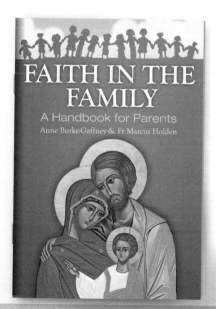

PA18 ISBN 978 1 86082 860 7

Hope in Adversity

Vima Dasan, SJ

This book gives guidance and encouragement to those going through a period of suffering. It offers the Word of God from Scripture as a divine source of inspiration, light and hope, together with writings from popular spiritual masters, and thoughtful reflections. It reflects on Faith, Patience, Prayer, Trust, Obedience and Hope in suffering. This little book of comfort counsels us not to fear, but to make a companion of wisdom, to pray confidently to the loving Father, to trust in God's will in the everyday things, and to live with courageous hope.

D656   ISBN 978 1 86082 148 6

Being a Parent Today

Edited by Fr Stephen Wang

Being a parent today is a huge privilege and a daunting challenge. It raises so many questions about how to love your children, how to live your family life, and how to pass on your Catholic faith. This booklet gathers together the experiences of different mothers, fathers, teachers and priests. It is not a list of rules, but a collection of ideas and practical suggestions that will help you reflect on your vocation as a parent and draw closer to your children.

PA16   ISBN 978 1 86082 786 0